Here Come the Girl Scouts!

The Amazing All-true Story of Juliette "Daisy" Gordon Low and Her Great Adventure

By **Shana Corey** Illustrated by **Hadley Hooper**

Scholastic Press / New York

To make yourself strong and healthy it is necessary to begin with your inside.

Daisy was a girl with gumption.

It is possible for any girl...to make herself into a strong and healthy

Daisy grew up in Savannah, Georgia, at a time when **proper** young ladies were supposed to be **dainty** and **delicate**.

woman if she takes the trouble to do few body exercises every day.

But Daisy came from a family of pathfinders and pioneers. She wanted **adventure** and **excitement**!

Fresh air is your great friend.

Delicate? thought Daisy.

Bosh!

How boring!

When Daisy grew up, she went traveling, ready for **adventure!** But on a visit home, she got an ear infection and lost almost all of her hearing. Daisy didn't let an obstacle stop her from seeing the world, though.

Her mother worried, so Daisy wrote and reassured her:

WELCOME ALL OBSTACLES, AS IT IS ONLY BY MEETING WITH DIFFICULTIES THAT YOU CAN KNOW HOW TO OVERCOME THEM, AND BE PREPARED FOR OTHERS IN THE FUTURE.

WARWICKSHIRE
MY 6
87

INLAND REVENUE
ONE PENNY

Progress, Daisy's Hearing
February 1st, heard a fog horn.
March 1st, hearing improved,
heard a camel when it rose.
April 1st, hearing decidedly
improved. Heard...grass growing.

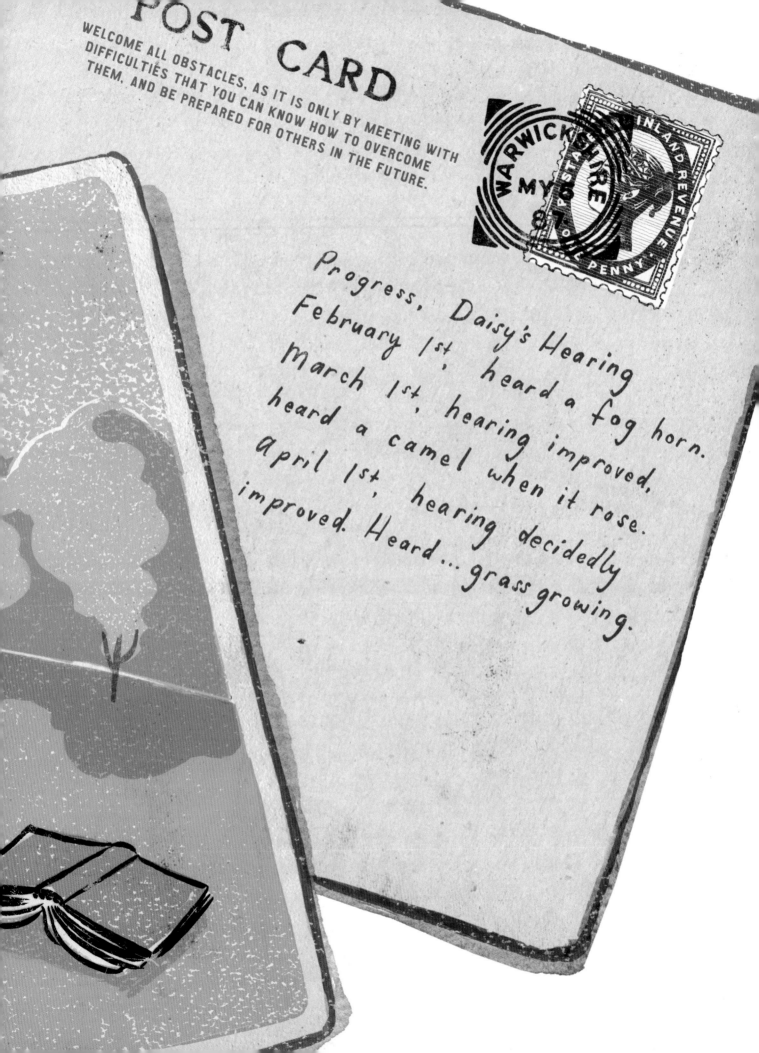

Daisy had adventure after adventure. When she wanted a new gate for her house, she took lessons from a blacksmith and forged it herself.

Every time you show your courage

She rode elephants in India, visited the Great Pyramid in Egypt,

it grows.

went fishing
during fancy
dinner parties,

and even flew in a monoplane.
"A delicious experience," she said.

After many years, though, Daisy grew restless. Her family had settled towns and served in wars, written books and built railroads. Daisy wanted more than adventure. She wanted to be **useful**, to make a **difference** in the world. But what could SHE do?

Then one day, Daisy discovered a group in England called the Boy Scouts. It had begun as a way for boys to help serve their country. And the Boy Scouts spent lots of time outdoors — running and camping and swimming and fishing. There was even a sister group called the Girl Guides. The more Daisy learned, the more excited she grew.

Why, the girls in America should have something like this!

Daisy thought.

Many of the greatest movements for the good of people, and

those which have influenced the WORLD most, have BEEN the work of one person.

Daisy couldn't wait to get started! She packed a Girl Guide handbook and took a steamer back home. When she arrived, she telephoned her cousin Nina. "Come right over!" she said. "I've got something for the girls of Savannah and all America and all the world and we're going to start it tonight!"

On March 12, 1912, Daisy began her biggest adventure yet! She invited eighteen girls to the first Girl Scout meeting. She told them about all the adventures they would have. They'd hike and camp and swim! They'd do good deeds. They'd learn to tie knots and survive in the wilderness and even save lives!

Getting right down and smelling the fresh soil is good for any one.

The girls thought Daisy's idea was **brilliant!** Daisy divided them into two troops. Then she taught them the ten Girl Scout laws.

From then on, Daisy devoted all her energy to the Girl Scouts.

She designed uniforms for them to wear.

She gave them her carriage house to meet in.

She turned the vacant lot across the street from her house
into a basketball court.

She even gave the Girl Scouts a boat so they could take
trips up and down the river.

Whatever you take up, do it with all your might

Daisy wanted the Girl Scouts to be open to lots of different girls, so she organized troops in private schools and in orphanages, in churches and in synagogues, in factories and in shops.

Of course, SOME people didn't approve of Daisy's new adventure. "Here come the Girl Scouts," they grumbled.

Unthinkable!

Preposterous!

But nothing would stop Daisy!

A Girl Scout Is a Friend to All, and a Sister to every Other Girl Scout No Matter to what Social Class she May Belong.

Daisy and her friend Professor Walter Hoxie worked together to write a handbook for the Girl Scouts. The girls read the book and learned all sorts of **interesting** things, such as:

How to find the time by the stars or by the sun.

How to cure hams.

How to secure a burglar with eight inches of cord.

Waste of time is the worst of waste. We can never get those moments back again.

How to stop a runaway horse.

How to brush your teeth
if a crocodile takes your
toothbrush.

How to get the skin
off a sardine.

The Girl Scouts worked on earning badges.

DAIRY MAID

NATURALIST

HORSEMANSHIP

PIONEER

SWIMMER

You will not have any luck unless you try hard.

INTERPRETER

CYCLIST

FLYER

To get the full benefit of actual contact with Nature breath of heaven can reach you and all wild things

The Girl Scouts went camping.

They took an oyster boat to an island near Savannah.

They sang songs around the campfire.

They feasted on fish and cornbread and turtle eggs.

At night, they tiptoed out of their tents and slept under the stars.

In this
United States
of ours we have cut
down too many trees...
So let us
plant trees.

Most of all, the Girl Scouts went on walks.

They savored the green.

They soaked up the sunshine.

They breathed the good fresh air.

All over Savannah, people saw the Girl Scouts swimming and singing, hiking and camping and playing basketball.

Some of them just sniffed and shook their heads. "Nature. Fresh air. Blech!" said one dainty damsel.

"In MY day, young ladies knew their place!" grouched a grandmamma.

"All that exercise can't be good for them," worried the neighbors.

When mean girls want you to join in some low fun, when you think it is not right...

Other people saw them, though, and cheered.

"Here come the Girl Scouts!"

They hugged their daughters and smiled and said,

"It's about time."

be brave, and have courage to say it isn't right. You will feel twice as happy afterwards.

Daisy traveled all over giving speeches
and raising money for the Girl Scouts.
Many people who heard her started
their own troops. Soon there were
Girl Scouts across the country.

The world looks to great organizations like the Girl Scouts

to break down ... petty barriers of race and class.

But Daisy never forgot the Girl Scouts of Savannah.

Whenever she wasn't traveling, she visited them and told them about her adventures. She shared stories of female doctors and scientists, architects and airplane pilots. And she read to them from the Girl Scout handbook: "One of you . . . may some day alter the lives of hundreds of thousands of people."

Daisy believed that girls could do anything.

REBECCA LOBO
Athlete

NATALIE MERCHANT
Musician

LISA LING
Journalist

LUCILLE BALL
Actor

Every little girl...   goes to make up

And she was right. Girl Scouts have been making a difference ever since — just like **DAISY.**

GLORIA STEINEM
Activist

HILLARY CLINTON
Politician

RITA DOVE
Poet

YOU

Some part or parcel of our great whole nation.

Growing up, I loved hearing my mom's tales of being a Girl Scout in Savannah, Georgia, in the 1960s.

As an adult, I've written picture books about women like Girl Scout founder Juliette Gordon Low (who was always called Daisy) — women with gumption, who weren't afraid to forge their own paths in the world. And so, with my mom's stories echoing in my head, I began to research Daisy. The more I learned, the more enamored I became, both of Daisy's own irresistibly eccentric personality and of the Girl Scouts themselves — an organization that embraced girl power and being green generations before either term was coined.

Daisy was born in Savannah on October 31, 1860. At age twenty-four, she lost partial hearing in one ear after a botched earache treatment. The following year, she married an Englishman, William Mackay Low. After the wedding ceremony, a grain of good-luck rice landed in her other ear, which led to an infection and an unsuccessful operation that eventually left her deaf in that ear.

Daisy was never afraid to be entirely herself, and the stories about her are legendary: She once snuck out of a fancy dinner party to go fishing in full evening dress with her friend Rudyard Kipling. She insisted on driving on the right side of the road in England (because she was American!) and on the left side of the road in America (because she was English!).

This portrait of Daisy as a young woman hangs in the Smithsonian's National Portrait Gallery. It was painted in 1887, soon after she married and moved to England.

When her camellias didn't bloom in time for a party, she "borrowed" blossoms from her neighbors' gardens and tied them to her trees! Children adored Daisy and she adored them, but adults didn't always approve of her eccentric ways.

The Progressive Era

Between 1890 and the 1920s, a fervor for reform known as the Progressive Era swept the United States. Women were at the forefront of this movement, organizing hundreds of clubs that worked toward everything from self-improvement to broad social change. During this time, Daisy began searching for something to give her own life meaning. She found it in 1911 when she met Sir Robert Baden-Powell, a Boer War hero who had founded the Boy Scouts in Great Britain. His sister, Agnes Baden-Powell, had organized an offshoot called the Girl Guides. Both groups encouraged citizenship and a love of the outdoors. Daisy quickly realized the possibilities such an organization had for American girls.

Daisy returned to Savannah the following spring. She was fifty-one years old and had never done any kind of major organizing in her life. But with her characteristic refusal to see obstacles, she forged ahead. On March 12, 1912, she invited eighteen girls to the first Girl Guide meeting (the name was changed to Girl Scouts in 1913). Daisy's niece was the first registered member, although she was out of town on March 12 and did not attend that first meeting.

Conservation

From the start, the Girl Scouts were required to do a good turn to someone every day, and meetings usually included a rousing game of tennis or basketball (a canvas curtain was strung up around the court so that passersby couldn't get a peek at the girls in their bloomers). The Girl Scouts also embraced the conservation movement, which was just beginning to take hold in America. (The Sierra Club was founded in 1892. And Theodore Roosevelt, considered the first conservation president, was elected in 1901.)

Much of the Girl Scouts' early connection to conservation can be credited to W. J. Hoxie, a naturalist who wrote for the *Savannah Morning News*. He led the first Girl Scouts on nature walks. And he, with Daisy's guidance, adapted the English Girl Guide manual into the first Girl Scout handbook, *How Girls Can Help Their Country* (1913). Most of the quotes that appear in the artwork of this book are from that handbook.

Diversity

Daisy had originally funded the Girl Scouts herself, but as their numbers grew, she began traveling to raise awareness and money for the movement. By all accounts, her methods (such as simply refusing to hear "no") were unconventional, but they worked. By 1920, there were nearly 70,000 Girl Scouts across the country. By the end of that decade, there were 200,000!

From the beginning, Daisy felt strongly that Girl Scouts should be for all girls. While the first troop was made up primarily of society girls, the daughters of dockworkers and locksmiths were soon joining as well. Daisy and the women who worked with her looked across class and religious lines and actively sought to form troops in orphanages, churches, and synagogues. They visited shops and factories to encourage young girls working there to join.

By 1917, the Girl Scouts had a monthly magazine, the *Rally*, which proudly noted that two Girl Scout troops had just been commissioned in Hawaii. Photographs from as early as 1920 show African American Girl Scouts in New York City. By 1921, the Girl Scouts officially opened to minorities, and there was soon a Chinese American troop in New York City's Chinatown, a Native American troop with girls from Onondaga Nation in New York State, and a Mexican American troop in Houston, Texas. Early troops were, for the most part, segregated, but by 1956 the Girl Scouts took their commitment to all girls a step further and launched a national drive to desegregate all troops.

The Legacy

Daisy Low believed she could do anything she set her mind to, and she believed the same thing was true for her Girl Scouts. Time and time again, the Girl Scouts have proven her right. Today, there are more than 3.2 million Girl Scouts in the United States and in more than ninety countries. Girl Scout alums have led the way for women in the arts, politics, science, sports, and women's rights. They've walked in space and won gold at the Olympics. There's even a Troop Capitol Hill, made up of Girl Scout alums in Congress.

Some things have changed since Daisy's time. In the 1930s, the popular cookie sale was introduced. Girl Scout uniforms are now green instead of blue. And, of course, Girl Scouts no longer spend much time stopping runaway horses or eating turtle eggs. The important things, though, have remained the same. Girl Scouts still learn the Girl Scout Promise and the Girl Scout Law. They hike and camp and do good turns to others. And most of all, one hundred years and counting after Daisy's first meeting, Girl Scouts continue to unite, inspire, and empower girls.

THE GIRL SCOUT PROMISE

On my honor, I will try:
To serve God and my country,
To help people at all times,
And to live by the Girl Scout Law.

COURTESY OF THE GEORGIA HISTORICAL SOCIETY

Daisy (center, with hat) and Savannah Girl Scouts enjoying the outdoors, approximately 1913.

THE GIRL SCOUT LAW

I will do my best to be
honest and fair,
friendly and helpful,
considerate and caring,
courageous and strong, and
responsible for what I say and do,
and to
respect myself and others,
respect authority,
use resources wisely,
make the world a better place, and
be a sister to every Girl Scout.

SOURCES

To find out more about the early Girl Scouts:
• Read the first handbook: Hoxie, W. J. *How Girls Can Help Their Country: Handbook for Girl Scouts.* Bedford, MA: Applewood Books, 2001. Originally published by Juliette Low in 1913.
• Visit the Girl Scout Museum and Archives at the Girl Scout Headquarters in New York City. www.girlscouts.org.
• Tour the Juliette Gordon Low Birthplace in Savannah, Georgia. www.juliettegordonlowbirthplace.org.

The following sources were also helpful in researching this book:
• Addington, Sarah. "The First Girl Scout." *Good Housekeeping*, February 1937.
• Burns, Olive Ann. "The Lady Who Started Girls' Lib." *Atlanta Journal and Constitution Magazine*, March 12, 1972.
• "Camping with Girl Scouts." *Rally*, Vol. 1, No. 10, July 1918.
• Dickson, Ted, Jr. "An International Movement Is the Organization of Girl Scouts, Which, Organized by Mrs. Low, Has Extended to Several Countries." *Savannah Morning News*, May 7, 1916.
• "The First Girl Scout Camp. Warsaw Island — July 8–18, 1913. Reminiscences of Mildred Guckenheimer Abrahams Kuhr." Courtesy of Temple Mickve Israel, Savannah, Georgia.
• Girl Scouts. *Scouting for Girls: Official Handbook of the Girl Scouts.* New York: Girl Scouts, 1920.
• Hochman, Anndee. "Pioneer Scout Shares Lessons." *Washington Post*, August 26, 1984.
• Lyon, Nancy. "Juliette Low: The Eccentric Who Founded the Girl Scouts." *Ms.*, November 1981.
• McAlpin, Sallie Margaret. "Memoirs of the Formative Days of Girl Scouts." *Savannah Morning News*, October 13, 1937.
• Pape, Nina Anderson. "Some Memories of a Charter Member of the Girl Scouts." *Savannah Morning News*, October 13, 1937.
• Seiler, Margaret M. "My Aunt, Juliette Gordon Low." *Leader*, Fall 2002.
• Shultz, Gladys Denny, and Daisy Gordon Lawrence. *Lady from Savannah: The Life of Juliette Low.* Philadelphia: Lippincott, 1958.

The quotes in this book were drawn from the above sources as follows:
• page 3 (in art): "To make yourself . . ." (Hoxie, 70)
• pages 4–5 (in art): "It is possible . . ." (Hoxie, 76)
• page 7 (in art): "Fresh air is . . ." (Hoxie, 66)
• page 9 (in art): "Welcome all obstacles . . ." (Hoxie, 117), "Progress, Daisy's Hearing . . ." (Schultz, 290–291)
• pages 10–11 (in art): "Every time you . . ." (Hoxie, 109)
• page 11 (in text): "A delicious experience" (Schultz, 326)
• pages 12–13 (in art): "Many of the . . ." (Hoxie, 117)
• page 14 (in art): "The work of . . ." (Hoxie, 103–104)
• page 15 (in text): "Come right over! . . ." (Burns, 9)
• page 16 (in art): "Getting right down . . ." (Hoxie, 63)
• page 18 (in art): "Whatever you take . . ." (Hoxie, 112)
• page 21 (in art): "A Girl Scout . . ." (Hoxie, 5)
• page 22 (in art): "Waste of time . . ." (Hoxie, 110)
• page 24 (in art): "You will not . . ." (Hoxie, 113)
• pages 26–27 (in art): "To get the . . ." (Hoxie, 19)
• page 28 (in art): "In this United States . . ." (Hoxie, 63)
• pages 30–31 (in art): "When mean girls . . ." (Hoxie, 109)
• pages 32–33 (in art): "The world looks . . ." (*Scouting for Girls*, 6–7)
• page 34 (in art): "To get on . . ." (*Rally*, 2)
• page 35 (in text): "One of you . . ." (Hoxie, 117)
• pages 36–37 (in art): "Every little girl . . ." (Hoxie, 17)

ACKNOWLEDGMENTS

This book would not have been possible without the help of a great many gutsy women with gumption. My heartfelt thanks to Pamela Cruz and Yevgeniya Gribov at the Girl Scout National Historic Preservation Center for sharing their extensive knowledge with me; to Donna Schneiderman, coleader of Brooklyn's Junior troop #2611, for introducing herself when she spotted me reading a biography of Juliette Gordon Low on a New York City subway and then connecting me with Margaret Seiler; to Margaret Seiler, Daisy Low's grandniece, for generously sharing her time and family stories; to Charisse Meloto, Marijka Kostiw, Emellia Zamani, and my amazing editor, Tracy Mack, at Scholastic Press for their endless enthusiasm, talent, and vision (Tracy, I knock on wood every time I think of you); and to Tracey Adams at Adams Literary Agency for her support and humor. Special thanks to Katherine Knapp Keena and Fran Powell Harold at the Juliette Gordon Low Birthplace in Savannah, Georgia, for their time and expertise in reviewing this manuscript, and especially to Katherine for her passion for history. Any mistakes that remain are entirely my own.

Thanks also to the wonderful librarians at the Georgia Historical Society and the Chatham County Public Library, and to my parents, Michael and Beverly Corey (who thought nothing of heading down to Savannah for a weekend of research when needed). And, most of all, thank you to my family — Pio, Jack, and Nate Alberto — the heart of everything I do.

To my favorite Girl Scout —
my mom, Beverly Klein Corey.
— SC

To Emma, Paige, and Abigail —
three girls with gumption!
— HH

LIBRARY OF CONGRESS CATALOGING-IN-PUBLICATION DATA AVAILABLE
ISBN 978-0-545-34278-0
10 9 8 7 6 5 4 3 2 1   12 13 14 15 16
Printed in Singapore   46
First edition, January 2012
The text type was set in Mrs. Eaves.
The display type was set in CircusMouseBook.
The illustrations were created with traditional paint, ink, and printmaking techniques, then scanned and assembled in Photoshop.
Art direction and book design by Marijka Kostiw

Green

Eggs and

ham